TEST YOUR CHILD

French

Headway · Hodder & Stoughton

Note for parents and teachers

Most French course books published at present are 'topic' based and put the emphasis in the early stages on learning phrases and expressions so that pupils can express themselves in particular situations in the foreign country. Some pupils need and appreciate supplementary explanations of how the language is structured. This book complements, while in no way replacing, the kind of course book described above for pupils in their first or second year of learning French. Simple explanations of basic grammar are given, followed by exercises. There is a French–English vocabulary at the back of the book and pupils should be encouraged to look up words they do not recognise in the vocabulary or in a good dictionary, such as *Harrap's First French Dictionary*.

Contents

This Headway edition first published 1990
by Hodder and Stoughton Educational,
a division of Hodder and Stoughton Ltd,
Mill Road, Dunton Green, Sevenoaks, Kent

ISBN 0 340 52718 8

Copyright © 1984 Marie-France Cavell

Printed and bound in Great Britain by
CW Print Group, Loughton, Essex.

Note for students

All languages have patterns and this book will show you some of the patterns in the French language. The following notes will help you to make the best use of this book.

1 Look up any French word you do not know in the French–English vocabulary at the back of the book. It is in alphabetical order. If the word is not there or if you wish to look up an English word, use a French–English dictionary. Your school library will probably have several or you might buy one for yourself.

2 Keep a vocabulary book in which you can write down any new word you come across. Always note down whether it is masculine or feminine.

3 Check the pronunciation of words you are unsure of with your teacher.

4 If you are sure of the pronunciation, practise the exercises with your parent or friend.

5 Learn patterns of words off by heart, such as: mon, ma, mes

6 The answers to the exercises are on page 31.

7 Do you know the meaning of these words? You will need to understand them to use this book.

    vowel – one of the letters a, e, i, o, u. The letter y can also be used as a vowel
    consonant – all the letters of the alphabet that are not vowels
    noun – a word used to name someone or something:
        Jane, Manchester, daffodil, boy, mouse
    verb – a word used to show an action: play, go, think
        or a state: be, have, seem
    singular – referring to one: girl
    plural – referring to more than one: girls
    negative – not doing, having or being something:
        She is not sleeping. We have no apples.
    infinitive – the part of the verb that means to do the action:
        to have, to be, to sell, to understand
    adjective – a word that describes a noun:
        hungry, greedy, sick, large

Le, la, l'

Nouns in French are either masculine or feminine. The word for the with masculine nouns is le and with feminine nouns is la. Here are some examples:

le mari	the husband	la femme	the wife/woman
le fils	the son	la fille	the daughter/girl
le père	the father	la mère	the mother
le cousin	the male cousin	la cousine	the female cousin
le grand-père	the grandfather	la grand-mère	the grandmother

It is easy to see why these nouns are masculine or feminine but with most nouns it is not so obvious. Look at this list:

le cheval	the horse	la souris	the mouse
le couteau	the knife	la fourchette	the fork
le jardin	the garden	la maison	the house

You must learn whether a noun is masculine or feminine the first time you come across it. In most dictionaries an *m.* after the noun tells us that it is masculine and an *f.* that it is feminine. Turn to the vocabulary at the back of this book and you will see that the nouns are followed by *m.* or *f.*

If a noun begins with a vowel, le and la are replaced by l' to make the noun easier to say. As h is not pronounced in French, the same rule usually applies to nouns beginning with h. Here are some examples:

l'hôpital *m.*	the hospital	l'ambulance *f.*	the ambulance
l'estomac *m.*	the stomach	l'oreille *f.*	the ear
l'agent *m.*	the policeman	l'actrice *f.*	the actress
l'argent *m.*	the money	l'école *f.*	the school

Put a circle round the correct word for the in the list below and write the English beside it.

A 1 le la (l') hôpital ...... *the hospital* ....

2 le la l' tête ....

3 le la l' argent ....

4 le la l' cheval ....

5 le la l' ambulance ....

6 le la l' agent ....

Label these pictures.

B 1 *le cheval* 2 .... 3 .... 4 .... 5 ....

Les

The word for the in front of all plural nouns is les. It makes no difference at all whether they are masculine or feminine nouns or whether they begin with a vowel. Look at the lists below:

le vélo	the bicycle	les vélos	the bicycles
l'agent	the policeman	les agents	the policemen
la voiture	the car	les voitures	the cars
l'actrice	the actress	les actrices	the actresses

Write the correct word at the end of the following sentences.

A 1 In front of a masculine singular noun the word for the is ....

2 In front of a feminine singular noun the word for the is ....

3 In front of a singular noun beginning with a vowel the word for the is ....

4 In front of all plural nouns the word for the is ....

Most nouns form the plural by adding -s, as above.
If a noun already ends in -s, -x or -z, it remains unchanged in the plural.

le fils	the son	les fils	the sons
le nez	the nose	les nez	the noses
la voix	the voice	les voix	the voices

Nouns ending in -au or -eu usually add -x in the plural.

| le couteau | the knife | les couteaux | the knives |
| le feu | the fire | les feux | the fires |

Nouns ending in -al usually drop the l and add -ux.

| le cheval | the horse | les chevaux | the horses |
| l'hôpital | the hospital | les hôpitaux | the hospitals |

Complete the following list.

B 1 le mari les *Maris* 5 la .... les femmes

2 le fils les .... 6 la fille les ....

3 le .... les pères 7 la souris les ....

4 le .... les couteaux 8 la .... les voix

Label these pictures. Sometimes you must write the noun in the singular and sometimes in the plural.

C 1 *les couteaux* 2 .... 3 .... 4 .... 5 ....

Un, une

The French word for a or an with a masculine noun is un and with a feminine singular noun une. Here are some examples:

le chien	the dog	un chien	a dog
le chat	the cat	un chat	a cat
l'oiseau *m*.	the bird	un oiseau	a bird
la vache	the cow	une vache	a cow
la poule	the hen	une poule	a hen
l'araignée *f*.	the spider	une araignée	a spider

Can you see the pattern? A le noun is an un noun and a la noun is an une noun. If the noun begins with a vowel, we have to find out whether it is masculine or feminine. In the list above oiseau is masculine and araignée is feminine, so we say un oiseau but une araignée

Fill in the gaps in the list below.

A 1 ...*le*... disque   the record   un disque   a record

   2 le livre   the book   .... livre   a book

   3 .... raquette   the racket   une raquette   a racket

   4 l'oreille   the ear   .... oreille   an ear

   5 l'agent   the policeman   .... agent   a policeman

   6 .... stylo   the pen   un stylo   a pen

Qu'est-ce que c'est? This question means What is it? To answer it you say   C'est un ....or   C'est une ....with the correct noun.

Qu'est-ce que c'est?   What is it?
C'est un nez.   It's a nose.

Point to these pictures and ask your parent or friend to give the correct answer. Practise on your own and when you are sure write your answer.

B 1 Qu'est-ce que c'est?   3 Qu'est-ce que c'est?

   C'est *un disque*.   C'est ....

   2 Qu'est-ce que c'est?   4 Qu'est-ce que c'est?

   C'est ....   C'est ....

1

2

3

4

Des

Des means some. Look at the list below.

un bonbon	a sweet	des bonbons	some sweets
un animal	an animal	des animaux	some animals
une orange	an orange	des oranges	some oranges
une pomme	an apple	des pommes	some apples

Un or une are used with singular nouns and des with plural nouns.

	Singular				Plural	
	masculine	feminine	m. or f. starting with a vowel		masculine	feminine
The	le	la	l'		les	les
A/an	un	une	un/une	Some	des	des

Write the English for the following words.

A 1 la vache *the cow*

5 le mari ....

2 un agent ....

6 un oiseau ....

3 des disques ....

7 des chiens ....

4 une maison ....

8 des bonbons ....

Change the following singular words into the plural.

B 1 le chien *les chiens*

5 l'oreille ....

2 le père ....

6 un nez ....

3 une vache ....

7 la tête ....

4 l'oiseau ....

8 l'école ....

Draw the picture to fit the labels below.

C 1 la maison   2 des chats   3 un cheval

4 une voiture   5 des araignées   6 des pieds

un, deux, trois

1 un/une	21 vingt et un	71 soixante et onze
2 deux	22 vingt-deux	72 soixante-douze
3 trois	23 vingt-trois	73 soixante-treize
4 quatre	24 vingt-quatre	74 soixante-quatorze
5 cinq	25 vingt-cinq	75 soixante-quinze
6 six	26 vingt-six	76 soixante-seize
7 sept	27 vingt-sept	77 soixante-dix-sept
8 huit	28 vingt-huit	78 soixante-dix-huit
9 neuf	29 vingt-neuf	79 soixante-dix-neuf
10 dix	30 trente	80 quatre-vingts
11 onze	40 quarante	81 quatre-vingt-un
12 douze	50 cinquante	82 quatre-vingt-deux
13 treize	60 soixante	90 quatre-vingt-dix
14 quatorze	70 soixante-dix	91 quatre-vingt-onze
15 quinze		92 quatre-vingt-douze
16 seize		100 cent
17 dix-sept		101 cent un
18 dix-huit	31, 41, 51 and 61 are formed in the same way as 21.	
19 dix-neuf	22, 33 etc. need a hyphen	
20 vingt	Note that **quatre**-vingts (80) ends in -s but **quatre-vingt-deux** etc. has no -s.	

Learn these numbers and you will be able to write almost any number.

Fill in the numbers below following the pattern set for 20–29.

A 30 *trente*   35 ....

31 ....   36 ....

32 ....   37 ....

33 ....   38 ....

34 ....   39 ....

Write the French words for the following numbers.

B 1 23 *vingt - trois*   5 70 ....

2 34 ....   6 79 ....

3 45 ....   7 87 ....

4 51 ....   8 94 ....

Avoir

Avoir means to have. It is the infinitive of the verb. Here is the verb written out in full:

j'ai	I have	nous avons	we have
tu as	you have	vous avez	you have
il a	he has	ils ont	they have (*m.*)
elle a	she has	elles ont	they have (*f.*)
on a	one has		

There are two words in French for you: tu and vous.

We use tu when talking to a child or to someone we know very well indeed, such as friends, parents, pets or close members of the family. We use vous when talking to more than one person at a time, or to someone we don't know very well, or to a person to whom we must be respectful.

Which word for you should be used in the following cases?

A　1　You are talking to your headmistress. ....*vous*................

　　2　You are talking to your brother. ....

　　3　You are talking to the person behind the Post Office counter. ....

　　4　Your teacher is telling all the pupils to open their books. ....

Look at these sentences:

Michel a un chien.　　　　　　　　Nous avons un chat.
Anne a deux lapins.　　　　　　　　As-tu un animal?

The verb avoir is used in each sentence. The first three are easy.

Michael has a dog.　　　　　　　　We have a cat.
Anne has two rabbits.

In the last sentence, as and tu are back to front. The last sentence says:

Have you an animal?

We can make similar questions with other parts of the verb.

Ai-je un frère?　　　　Have I a brother?
A-t-il un chat?　　　　Has he a cat?
A-t-elle un chien?　　　Has she a dog?
Avons-nous l'argent?　　Have we the money?
Avez-vous une sœur?　　Have you a sister?
Ont-ils des glaces?　　　Have they any ice-creams?

We need a hyphen when we change the verb round and in the case of il and elle we need a hyphen, a t, and another hyphen: a-t-il, a-t-elle. The words are easier to say like that.

Here is a picture of Marie with her birthday presents. Make a sentence to name each present.

B   1 ....

    2 ....

    3 ....

    4 ....

    5 ....

Now answer these questions about her presents, either oui (yes) or non (no).

C   1 A-t-elle une radio? ..*non*..   3 A-t-elle deux disques? ....

    2 A-t-elle des bonbons? ....   4 A-t-elle un vélo? ....

Instead of non as your answer to question 4 you could have written:
   Elle n'a pas de vélo. She hasn't a bike.

To change 'she has a bike' to 'she hasn't a bike' we:
   put n' (short for ne) in front of the a;
   put pas after the a;
   change un to de. Similarly we would change une or des to de.
Here are some more examples:

Je n'ai pas de chat.	I haven't a cat.
Tu n'as pas de voiture.	You haven't a car.
Il n'a pas de frère.	He hasn't a brother.
Nous n'avons pas de radio.	We haven't a radio.
Vous n'avez pas de bonbons.	You haven't any sweets.
Ils n'ont pas d'hôpital.	They haven't a hospital.

Change these sentences to make them negative. This means change them from saying that the people do have a certain object to saying that they do not have it.

D   1 Elle a une radio. .....*Elle n'a pas de radio*.....................

    2 Charles a un vélo. ....

    3 J'ai une glace. ....

    4 Nous avons un cousin. ....

10

Mon, ma, mes

When describing your family or things you own you need to be able to say my brother, my bike etc. This is how you do it:

You put mon in front of a masculine singular noun: mon frère

ma in front of a feminine singular noun: ma sœur

mon in front of a feminine singular noun
beginning with a vowel: mon amie (girl friend)

mes in front of all plural nouns: mes sœurs, mes frères

Put the correct word for my in front of the following nouns.

A   1 ...*ma*... maison   2 .... mère   3 .... frères   4 .... vélo

5 .... nez   6 .... oreilles   7 ....lapins   8 .... voiture

9 .... gâteaux

The same pattern of words exists for *your*, *his* and *her*.

my	mon frère	ma sœur	mes frères	mes sœurs
your	ton frère	ta sœur	tes frères	tes sœurs
his/her	son frère	sa sœur	ses frères	ses sœurs

Son, sa and ses mean both his and her. You can usually tell from the rest of the sentence which they mean. Here are some examples:

Voici Pierre et son amie.	Here are Pierre and **his** girl friend.
Annick a son vélo.	Annick has **her** bike.
Jean n'a pas son vélo.	Jean has not got **his** bike.

Write the French for the following words.

B   1 my brother ...*mon frère*...   5 my rabbits ....

2 his sister ....   6 my sisters ....

3 her husband ....   7 her father ....

4 your female cousins ....   8 my school ....

Did you get those right or did you make the mistake of writing sa père for question 7? Remember that the noun decides which word goes in front of it. Père is a masculine singular noun and so son is the correct word for her not sa. Did you also remember to write mon école for question 8. Remember that although école is a feminine singular noun and we might expect to use ma, we use mon instead because école begins with a vowel. Try a few more.

C   1 her ear ....   3 my girl friend ....

2 your school ....   4 her brothers ....

Notre, votre, leur

Ton, ta and tes are the words for your when we are using tu for you. When vous is being used, the words for your are votre and vos.

votre livre	your book	vos livres	your books
votre amie	your girl friend	vos amies	your girl friends

As you see, votre is used for all singular nouns and vos is used with all plural nouns, whether they are masculine or feminine, or begin with a vowel. The words for our and their follow the same pattern.

notre ami	our firned	nos amis	our friends
notre école	our school	nos écoles	our schools
leur hôtel *m.*	their hotel	leurs hôtels	their hotels
leur adresse *f.*	their address	leurs adresses	their addresses

You have now learnt the whole list of words showing possession. Learn the table below by saying it out loud over and over again. If you can learn it off by heart, you will always be able to remember the word you need.

	Singular		Plural
	masculine	feminine	
my	mon	ma	mes
your	ton	ta	tes
his/her	son	sa	ses
our	notre	notre	nos
your	votre	votre	vos
their	leur	leur	leurs

Underline the correct word in the exercise below.

A 1 his mother   son   sa   ses   mère

2 our sisters   notre   nos   sœurs

3 your brothers   votre   vos   frères

4 your dog   ton   ta   tes   chien

5 their garden   leur   leurs   jardin

6 your hotel   ton   ta   tes   hôtel

7 my address   mon   ma   mes   adresse

8 her husband   son   sa   ses   mari

9 our cat   notre   nos   chat

10 your mother   ton   ta   tes   mère

La famille

Voici un arbre généalogique.
Here is a family tree.

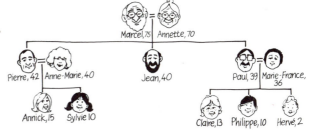

In French, age is expressed like this:

Annick a quinze ans. Annick is fifteen. (Annick has fifteen years.) To say
'I am twelve' you need: the correct part of avoir   J'ai

                    the correct number   douze

                    the word for years   ans.

Look at the family tree and complete these sentences, using words not figures.

A   1 Claire a ...._treize_....... ans.   3 Hervé a .... ans.

       2 Anne-Marie a .... ans.   4 Marcel a .... ans.

To ask a friend's age you say: Quel âge as-tu? How old are you?

                      or Quel âge a ton frère? How old is your brother?

Imagine that you are Philippe and answer the following questions.

B   1 Quel âge a ton frère?   ...._Il a deux ans_...............

       2 Quel âge a ta sœur? ....

       3 Quel âge a ta mère? ....

       4 Quel âge a ton oncle Jean? ....

       5 Quel âge ont tes cousines? ....

You may have a stepmother, stepfather, stepbrother or sister. Here are the words in French and a few more words for members of the family:

le beau-père	stepfather	la belle-mère	stepmother
le beau-frère	stepbrother	la belle-sœur	stepsister
le demi-frère	half-brother	la demi-sœur	half-sister

Answer the following questions about yourself.

C   1 Quel âge as-tu? ....

       2 As-tu des sœurs? ....

       3 As-tu des frères? ....

Adjectives

The masculine singular adjective meaning small is   petit
   to make the feminine singular adjective, add -e   petite
   to make the masculine plural adjective, add -s   petits
   to make the feminine plural adjective, add -es   petites
Here are some examples:

un petit cartable   une petite fille   deux petits livres   deux petites glaces

Here are some other adjectives that change in the same way.

grand	big; tall	mauvais	bad
joli	pretty	content	pleased
court	short	méchant	naughty, wicked
fâché	angry	laid	ugly
français	French	anglais	English

Choose the correct description from the list below for each picture.
une petite souris; un joli jardin; une jolie rose; une méchante petite fille

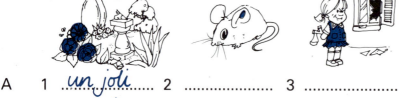

A   1   *un joli jardin*   2 ....   3 ....   4 ....

Choose the correct form of the adjective from the words in brackets.

B   1   une *petite* maison (petit, petite, petits, petites)

    2   deux .... écoles (grand, grande, grands, grandes)

    3   un .... hôtel (grand, grande, grands, grandes)

    4   deux .... garçons (méchant, méchante, méchants, méchantes)

Most adjectives go after the noun but some go before.
These adjectives always go before the noun.

joli	pretty	grand	big, tall
vieux	old	beau	beautiful
jeune	young	gros	big, fat
petit	small	large	wide
court	short	haut	high
gentil	nice, kind	excellent	excellent
long	long	meilleur	better

Sometimes adjectives form the feminine or the plural in ways other than those explained on the previous page. Look at the following examples.

	masc. sing.	fem. sing.	masc. plural	fem. plural
yellow	jaune	jaune	jaunes	jaunes
expensive	cher	chère	chers	chères
happy	heureux	heureuse	heureux	heureuses
fat	gros	grosse	gros	grosses
nice	gentil	gentille	gentils	gentilles
good	bon	bonne	bons	bonnes
white	blanc	blanche	blancs	blanches
long	long	longue	longs	longues
favourite	favori	favorite	favoris	favorites
equal	égal	égale	égaux	égales

Some adjectives have two forms of the masculine singular.

beautiful	beau/bel	belle	beaux	belles
new	nouveau/nouvel	nouvelle	nouveaux	nouvelles
old	vieux/vieil	vieille	vieux	vieilles

In these cases the alternative masculine singular form is used in front of a masculine singular noun beginning with a vowel or an -h. Again, this simply makes the words easier to say. Here are some examples:

un beau château	a beautiful castle
un **bel** hôtel	a beautiful hotel
un nouveau film	a new film
un **nouvel** électrophone	a new record player
un vieux grand-père	an old grandfather
un **vieil** homme	an old man

Look for the feminine forms of the adjectives in the following sentences and underline them.

C   1 un bel arbre   2 une bonne école   3 trois vieilles voitures
    4 mon livre favori   5 la nouvelle voiture   6 le vieil arbre

Write the following in French, remembering to check whether the adjective comes before or after the noun.

D   1 an old tree .... *un vieil arbre* ....

    2 an old woman ....

    3 her favourite record ....

    4 two beautiful apples ....

Être

Être is the verb meaning to be. Here it is written out in full:

je suis	I am	nous sommes	we are
tu es	you are	vous êtes	you are
il, elle, on est	he, she, it, one is	ils sont	they (*m.*) are
		elles sont	they (*f.*) are

This verb can be changed to make questions or negative statements just as the verb avoir can.

suis-je	am I?	je ne suis pas	I am not
es-tu?	are you?	tu n'es pas	you are not
est-il?	is he?	il n'est pas	he is not
est-elle?	is she?	elle n'est pas	she is not
sommes-nous?	are we?	nous ne sommes pas	we are not
êtes-vous?	are you?	vous n'êtes pas	you are not
sont-ils?	are they? (*m.*)	ils ne sont pas	they (*m.*) are not
sont-elles	are they? (*f.*)	elles ne sont pas	they (*f.*) are not

Note that in the question form est-il we do not need an extra -t as in a-t-il

Write the French for the following.

A 1 we are *nous sommes*   5 they (*m.*) are not ....

2 I am not ....   6 am I? ....

3 you are (pl.) ....   7 are we? ....

4 you are not (pl.) ....

Carole is describing the things in her room.

> Mon électrophone est nouveau. Il est très cher. J'ai vingt disques. Ils sont excellents. Mon petit chat est blanc. Il n'est pas méchant. J'ai une belle raquette. Elle est jaune et blanche. Mes livres sont grands et petits. Mon livre favori est *Astérix*. Ma radio n'est pas nouvelle. Elle est vieille.

If the following statements are correct, put a tick after them. If not, put a cross.

B 1 Carole's radio is new. ☒ 2 Her cat is black. ☐ 3 Her record player is old. ☐ 4 She has twenty records. ☐ 5 Her record player did not cost a lot. ☐ 6 She likes her records. ☐ 7 Her tennis racket is red and white. ☐ 8 Her cat is not naughty. ☐ 9 Her favourite book is Astérix. ☐ 10 Her racket is not a very nice one. ☐ 11 She has a big cat. ☐

Bleu, blanc, rouge

Colour in the squares.

		brun brown ☐	rose pink ☐
rouge red ☐	bleu blue ☐	blanc white ☐	noir black ☐
vert green ☐	jaune yellow ☐	gris grey ☐	orange orange ☐

No -e is added to the feminine form of jaune, rose or rouge. Look back to page 15 to remind yourself how blanc changes. Orange never changes, even when describing plural words.

Colour in the picture below following the instructions given.

A   Le vélo est rouge. Le ciel est bleu. Les arbres sont verts et bruns et les pommes sont vertes. Le chien est noir et blanc. Le chat est brun. La tente est orange. Les roses sont jaunes. La maison est grise.

Look at the following statements. If they are correct, put a tick in the box. If they are false, put a cross.

B   1 Le drapeau anglais est bleu, blanc et vert. [X] 2 Les bananes sont jaunes. ☐ 3 La neige est bleue. ☐ 4 Les ambulances sont blanches. ☐ 5 Les pommes sont grises. ☐ 6 Les vaches sont vertes. ☐ 7 Le ciel est bleu et gris. ☐ 8 Les disques sont noirs. ☐

Write the following phrases in French.

C   1 the white cat ...... *le chat blanc* ....

2 the brown cow ....

3 The French flag is red, blue and white. ....

....

4 The house is white and black. ....

Où

Où means where. Here are some words describing position:

dans	in	devant	in front of	sous	under
derrière	behind	entre	between	sur	on

Look at this picture. The sentences beside it describe where things are.

1 Le lit est entre la chaise et la commode.
2 Le chat est derrière l'armoire.
3 La raquette est sur le lit.
4 Les balles sont sous la chaise.
5 Les fleurs sont dans le vase.
6 Le lit est devant l'armoire.

Are the following sentences true or false? If they are true, write vrai (true) beside them. If not, write faux (false).

A   1 Le chat est devant l'armoire. ....*faux*...... 2 Le lit est derrière la

chaise. .... 3 Le vase est sur la commode. ....

4 Les fleurs sont dans le vase. ....

Look again at the picture above and answer the following questions.

B   1 Où est le lit? *Le lit est entre la chaise et la commode*

2 Où est l'armoire? ....

3 Où sont les balles? ....

4 Où est la raquette? ....

Complete the following sentences about the picture on the left.

C   1 Le panier est entre *la carafe d'eau et le verre*

2 Le vin est derrière ....

3 L'assiette est entre ....

4 Le sel et le poivre sont devant ....

....

assiette *f.* plate   bouteille *f.* bottle   carafe d'eau *f.* carafe of water
pain *m.* bread   panier *m..* basket   poivre *m.* pepper   sel *m.* salt
verre *m.* glass   vin *m.* wine.

18

Ce, cette, ces

In French we use the same word for this and that, but it has three forms.

ce goes in front of a masculine singular noun: ce garçon
this/that boy

cet goes in front of a masculine singular noun
that begins with a vowel: cet arbre
this/that tree

cette goes in front of a feminine singular noun: cette actrice
this/that actress

In the same way, those and these are the same word in French.

ces goes in front of all plural nouns: ces garçons these/those boys
ces filles   these/those girls
ces hommes these/those men

Draw a circle around the correct word for this or that, these or those.

A   1 ce cet cette (ces) garçons   5 ce cet cette ces hôpital

2 ce cet cette ces oreilles   6 ce cet cette ces cartables

3 ce cet cette ces lapin   7 ce cet cette ces ambulance

4 ce cet cette ces hommes   8 ce cet cette ces arbre

Write the French for the following.

B   1 this son ....*ce fils*...............   4 these houses ....

2 these daughters ....   5 this school ....

3 this hotel ....   6 these apples ....

Ce, cet and cette mean both this and that, but by adding -ci or -là to the noun, we can make quite sure that it is clear which is meant.

Ce livre-ci est petit.   Ce livre-là est grand.
This book is small.   That book is big.

Cette pomme-ci est dans le panier.   Cette pomme-là est sur la table.
This apple is in the basket.   That apple is on the table.

Those and these are formed in the same way: ces crayons-ci these pencils
ces crayons-là those pencils

– Er verbs

Avoir and être are irregular verbs. Most verbs, however, fit into a pattern. A very large number of verbs whose infinitive ends in -er follow the pattern shown below.

travailler to work	
je travaille	I work, I am working, I do work
tu travailles	you work, you are working, you do work
il, elle, on travaille	he, she, one works, is working, does work
nous travaillons	we work, we are working, we do work
vous travaillez	you work, your are working, you do work
ils, elles travaillent	they work, they are working, they do work

Look at the endings: -e, -es, -e, -ons, -ez, -ent.
To fit the endings, we remove the -er from the infinitive and replace it with the correct ending above. Learn the endings off by heart and you will be able to form any verb whose infinitive ends with -er.

Here are some more -er verbs: jouer to play; tricher to cheat; voler to fly; pêcher to fish; porter to carry; montrer to show; laver to wash; gagner to win; écouter to listen; regarder to look at.

je joue	I play, I am playing, I do play
tu triches	you cheat, you are cheating, you do cheat
il vole	he flies, he is flying, he does fly
nous pêchons	we fish, we are fishing, we do fish
vous portez	you carry, you are carrying, you do carry
elles gagnent	they win, they are winning, they do win

We can form questions and make negative statements just as we did with avoir and être:

je ne travaille pas   I don't work, I am not working
pêchez-vous?   are you fishing, do you fish?

Some -er verbs are a little peculiar.

1 These verbs add a grave accent è before silent endings. A grave accent is not added in the nous and vous forms because the ending is not silent. We can hear -ons and -ez but we cannot hear -e. Here is an example:

acheter to buy	
j'achète	nous achetons
tu achètes	vous achetez
il, elle, on achète	ils, elles achètent

Other examples of verbs that behave in this way are: mener to lead; lever to raise; espérer to hope; céder to give in; répéter to repeat; préférer to prefer.

2 These verbs add -e before -ons in the nous form. If the -e were not there the -g would sound like the -g in garden. Here is an example:

manger to eat	
je mange	nous mangeons
tu mange	vous mangez
il, elle, on mange	ils, elles mangent

Other verbs that behave in this way are: plonger to dive; nager to swim.

3 Verbs whose infinitive ends in -cer. These verbs soften the -c before -ons in the nous form with a cedilla -ç. If the cedilla were not there the -c would sound like the -c in cat instead of the -c in ceiling. Here is an example:

commencer to begin	
je commence	nous commençons
tu commences	vous commencez
il, elle, on commence	ils, elles commencent

Another example of a verb that behaves in this way is lancer to throw.

4 In the verbs appeler to call and jeter to throw the consonant is doubled before the silent endings.

je jette	nous jetons
tu jettes	vous jetez
il, elle, on jette	ils, elles jettent

5 In -oyer and -uyer verbs, the -y becomes -i before silent endings. Here are two examples:

nettoyer to clean	essuyer to wipe
je nettoie	j'essuie
tu nettoies	tu essuies
il, elle, on nettoie	il, elle, on essuie
nous nettoyons	nous essuyons
vous nettoyez	vous essuyez
ils, elles nettoient	ils, elles essuient

All of these changes make the words easier to say. The endings are always -e, -es, -e, -ons, -ez, -ent.

Exercises on -er verbs

Write out in full the verb regarder to look at and give the English meaning beside each part.

A   je ....

tu ....

il, elle, on ....

nous ....

vous ....

ils, elles ....

Draw a line between the French sentence and its English version.

B   1 Ils travaillent.   a Are you listening?
     2 Je ne triche pas.   b They are working.
     3 Elle joue.   c We are not washing.
     4 Écoutez-vous?   d She's playing.
     5 Nous ne lavons pas.   e I don't cheat.

Write the English for the following sentences.

C   1 Je jette la balle. ...*I throw the ball.*...

2 Nous commençons nos devoirs. ....

3 Il nettoie la maison. ....

4 Vous appelez le chat. ....

5 Elles essuient le tableau noir. ....

Qu'est-ce qu'il fait? This question means What is he doing? Look at the pictures and try to write what is happening in them.

D   1 ...*Elle joue.*...... 2 .... 3 ....

4 .... 5 ....

22

du, de la, de l', des, de, d'

All of these words mean some or any. In English there are times when we can miss out these words. We can say 'I eat sweets'. We do not have to say 'I eat some sweets'. But in French we must put in the word that means some or any.

du goes in front of a masculine singular noun: du pain   some bread

de la goes in front of a feminine singular noun: de la viande
some meat

de l' goes in front of a masculine or feminine noun
beginning with a vowel or silent -h: de l'essence (f.)
some petrol

des goes in front of a plural noun: des bonbons   some sweets

de and d' are used after a negative: je n'ai pas d'argent / de bonbons.
I have no money / sweets.

or before a plural adjective: j'ai de bons amis.
I have good friends.

Look at the pattern below.

	singular			plural
	masc.	fem.	masc. or fem. beginning with vowel	
some, any	du	de la	d'	des
	singular after negative			plural after negative
	de or d'			de or d'

Here are some more examples:

du café	coffee	de la limonade	lemonade
du chocolat	chocolate	de la bière	beer
du fromage	cheese	de la farine	flour
du jambon	ham	de la salade	salad
du sucre	sugar		
du thé	tea	des biscuits (m.)	biscuits
		des frites (f.)	chips
de l'eau (f.)	water	des oranges (f.)	oranges
de l'huile(f.)	oil		

Put either du, de la, de l', des, de or d' in front of the following nouns.

A   1 J'achète ...*du*... thé.   2 Il n'a pas .... argent.   3 Nous achetons

.... café.   4 Elle achète .... farine.   5 J'achète .... gâteaux.

6 As-tu .... bonbons?   7 Ma mère achète .... huile.   8 J'ai

.... fromage.   9 Ils n'ont pas .... fromage.   10 J'ai ....

jolies sœurs.

La ville

Look at the plan of a town (une ville) below. You should be able to tell what all the words mean from the pictures beside them but look up any you are not sure of in the vocabulary at the back of this book.

Here are some more words for indicating position:

à côté de	beside	en face de	opposite
au milieu de	in the middle of	près de	near to

The de changes according to the noun following it:

à côté du cinéma — next to the cinema
au milieu de la place — in the middle of the square
en face de l'alimentation générale — opposite the general store
près des magasins — near to the shops

Look again at the plan above. Are the following statements true? If so, write vrai next to them, if not, write the correct statement.

A 1 Le café est en face du cinéma. *vrai* ....

2 La papeterie est à côté de la boucherie. ....

3 Le parking est à côté de la pâtisserie. ....

4 La boulangerie est en face du syndicat d'initiative. ....

....

5 La statue est au milieu du supermarché. ....

6 Le supermarché est à côté de la pharmacie et de la boulangerie.

....

7 Le parking n'est pas près des magasins. ....

Du, de la, de l', des, de, d'

In English we can talk about possession in two ways: the boy's dog
the dog of the boy
In French the second way of expressing possession is the only way:
le chien du garçon

du means of the in front of masculine singular nouns:
le pantalon du garçon   the boy's trousers
de la means of the in front of feminine singular nouns:
la jupe de la jeune fille   the girl's skirt
de l' means of the in front of masculine or feminine nouns
beginning with a vowel or silent -h:
le chapeau de l'homme   the man's hat
le nom de l'école   the school's name
des means of the in front of all plural nouns:
les gants (m.) des garçons   the boys' gloves
les chaussures (f.) des jeunes filles   the girls' shoes
de and d' mean of not of the:
le chat de mon oncle   my uncle's cat
le chien d'Annick   Annick's dog

Put a circle around the correct word for of or of the in the following phrases.

A 1 les chaussures   du   de la   de l'   des   de   (d')   Anne
  2 les oreilles   du   de la   de l'   des   de   d'   chat
  3 le pantalon   du   de la   de l'   des   de   d'   jeune fille
  4 les disques   du   de la   de l'   des   de   d'   Charles
  5 la voiture   du   de la   de l'   des   de   d'   agent
  6 les chapeaux   du   de la   de l'   des   de   d'   amis
  7 le cartable   du   de la   de l'   des   de   d'   sœur

Write the following phrases in French.

B 1 the boy's cat ....*le chat du garçon*..........

  2 my sister's dog ....

  3 the men's cars ....

  4 the cat's ears ....

  5 Jean's ice-cream ....

  6 my friend's radio ....

Aller

Aller means to go and is an irregular verb. That is to say that like avoir and être it does not fit into a pattern. Here it is written in full:

je vais	I go, I do go, I am going
tu vas	you go, you do go, you are going
il, elle, on va	he, she, one goes, does go, is going
nous allons	we go, we do go, we are going
vous allez	you go, you do go, you are going
ils, elles vont	they go, they do go, they are going

When we use this verb, we usually say where we are going. There are four ways of saying to the in French.

au goes in front of a singular masculine noun: au cinéma to the cinema

à la goes in front of a singular feminine noun: à la place to the square

à l' goes in front of a masculine or feminine singular noun beginning with a vowel: à l'hôpital to the hospital

aux goes in front of all plural nouns: aux magasins to the shops

Look at the list of names on the left below and follow the lines that say where they are going. Then pretend to be each of those people in turn. In each case you must choose au, à la, à l' or aux. Here is an example:

Sylvie would say: Je vais aux magasins.

A
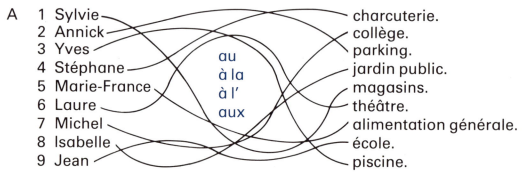

1 Sylvie — charcuterie.
2 Annick — collège.
3 Yves — parking.
4 Stéphane — jardin public.
5 Marie-France — magasins.
6 Laure — théâtre.
7 Michel — alimentation générale.
8 Isabelle — école.
9 Jean — piscine.

au
à la
à l'
aux

Fill in the correct form of the verb aller.

B 1 Nous *allons* à la gare.

2 Elles .... au collège.

3 Tu ne .... pas à l'hôpital.

4 Vous .... à la boulangerie.

5 On .... à la plage.

6 .... -tu à la place?

7 Il ne .... pas au cinéma.

8 Nous .... à la piscine.

Faire

Faire means to do or to make. It is an irregular verb.

je fais	I do	nous faisons	we do
tu fais	you do	vous faites	you do
il, elle, on fait	he, she, one does	ils, elles font	they do

Qu'est-ce que in front of these parts of the verb makes the question What are you doing? etc.

Qu'est-ce que je fais?   What am I doing?
Qu'est-ce qu'elles font?   What are they doing?

Here are some useful phrases containing the verb faire:

faire la vaisselle	to do the washing up
faire les courses (f.)	to do the shopping
faire les lits (m.)	to make the beds
faire les devoirs (m.)	to do homework
faire une promenade	to go for an outing

See how many others you can collect and write in your vocabulary book.

Faire is also used in phrases describing the weather:

Quel temps fait-il?	What is the weather like?		
Il fait beau.	It is fine.	Il fait mauvais.	The weather is bad.
Il fait du brouillard.	It is foggy.	Il fait du soleil.	It is sunny.
Il fait chaud.	It is hot.	Il fait du vent.	It is windy.
Il fait froid.	it is cold.		

The following weather expressions do not use faire but it is worth learning them at the same time.

Il gèle.	It is freezing.	Il neige.	It is snowing.	Il pleut.	It is raining.

Describe the weather in the pictures below.

A   1   *Il fait beau*.....   2   3   ....

Fill in the correct part of the verb faire.

B   1   Je *fais* la vaisselle.   2   Il ...... beau   3   Ils ...... les lits.

Quelle heure est-il?

Il est une heure.	It is one o'clock.
Il est deux heures cinq.	It is five past two.
Il est trois heures dix.	It is ten past three.
Il est quatre heures et quart.	It is a quarter past four.
Il est cinq heures vingt.	It is twenty past five.
Il est six heures vingt-cinq.	It is twenty-five past six.
Il est sept heures et demie.	It is half past seven.
Il est huit heures moins vingt-cinq.	It is twenty-five to eight.
Il est neuf heures moins vingt.	It is twenty to nine.
Il est dix heures moins le quart.	It is quarter to ten.
Il est onze heures moins dix.	It is ten to eleven.
Il est minuit moins cinq.	It is five minutes to midnight.
Il est midi.	It is midday.
Il est minuit.	It is midnight.

NB There is an -e on demie for every hour except twelve. We say:
Il est trois heures et demie. but Il est midi (minuit) et demi.
We say quatre heures et quart for quarter past four but
quatre heures moins le quart for quarter to four.

Quelle heure est-il? What time is it? Write the time in French beside these clocks.

A 1 *Il est une heure dix*

2 ....

3 ....

4 ....

5 ....

6 ....

The French use the twenty-four-hour clock. Where we would say one p.m., they say thirteen hours (treize heures).

1.00 p.m. treize heures	7.00 p.m. dix-neuf heures
2.00 p.m. quatorze heures	8.00 p.m. vingt heures
3.00 p.m. quinze heures	9.00 p.m. vingt et une heures
4.00 p.m. seize heures	10.00 p.m. vingt-deux heures
5.00 p.m. dix-sept heures	11.00 p.m. vingt-trois heures
6.00 p.m. dix-huit heures	

Practise saying the following times in French.
B   1 3.20 a.m.   2 6.30 p.m.   3 12 a.m.   4 4.45 p.m.   5 8.15 p.m.

French–English vocabulary

à   at, to
à côté de   beside
acheter   to buy
actrice f.   actress
adresse f.   address
âge m.   age
agent m.   policeman
alimentation générale f.
   food shop
aller   to go
ambulance f.
   ambulance
ami m.   friend
amie f.   girl friend
an m.   year
anglais   English
animal m.   animal
appeler   to call
araignée f.   spider
arbre m.   tree
argent m.   money
armoire f.   wardrobe
assiette f.   plate
au, aux   to the
au milieu de   in the
   middle of
avoir   to have

balle f.   ball
banane f.   banana
beau   fine, beautiful
beau-frère m.
   step-brother
beau-père m.
   step-father
belle-mère f.
   step-mother
belle-sœur f.
   step-sister
bière f.   beer
biscuit m.   biscuit
blanc   white
bleu   blue
bon   good
bonbon m.   sweet
boucherie f.   butcher's
   shop
boulangerie f.   baker's
   shop
bouteille f.   bottle
brun   brown

café m.   café, coffee

carafe f.   carafe
cartable m.   school bag
ce, cet, cette   this/that
céder   to give in
ces   these/those
chaise f.   chair
chapeau m.   hat
charcuterie f.   pork
   butcher's
chat m.   cat
château m.   castle
chaussure f.   shoe
cher   expensive, dear
cheval m.   horse
chien m.   dog
chocolat m.   chocolate
ciel m.   sky
cinéma m.   cinema
collège m.   secondary
   school
commencer   to begin
commode f.   dressing-
   table
content   happy, pleased
court   short
cousin m.   male cousin
cousine f.   female cousin
couteau m.   knife
crayon m.   pencil

dans   in
de   of
demi   half
demi-frère m.   half-brother
demi-sœur f.   half-sister
des   of the, some
derrière   behind
devant   in front of
devoirs m.   homework
disque m.   record
drapeau m.   flag
du   of the

eau f.   water
école f.   school
écouter   to listen
égal   equal
électrophone m.   record
   player
elle   she, it
elles   they (f.)
en face de   opposite
entre   between

et   and
être   to be
espérer   to hope
essence f.   petrol
essuyer   to wipe
estomac m.   stomach
excellent   excellent

fâché   angry
favori   favourite
faux   false
faire   to do, make
faire beau   to be fine
      weather;
   chaud   to be hot
      weather;
   du brouillard   to be
      foggy;
   du soleil   to be
      sunny;
   du vent   to be
      windy;
   froid   to be cold
      weather;
   la vaisselle   to do the
      washing up;
   les courses   to do the
      shopping;
   les devoirs   to do
      homework;
   mauvais   to be bad
      weather;
   une promenade   to
      go for an outing;
farine f.   flour
femme f.   woman, wife
feu m.   fire
fille f.   daughter, girl
film m.   film
fils m.   son
fleur f.   flower
fourchette f.   fork
français   French
frère m.   brother
frite f.   chip
fromage m.   cheese

gagner   to win
gant m.   glove
garçon m.   boy
gare f.   station
gâteau m.   cake
gentil   nice, kind

glace *f.* ice-cream
grand big, tall
grand-mère *f.* grand-mother
grand-père *m.* grand-father
gris grey
gros fat, large

haut high
heure *f.* hour, time
heureux fortunate, happy
homme *m.* man
hôpital *m.* hospital
hôtel *m.* hotel
huile *f.* oil

il he, it
il gèle it is freezing
il neige it is snowing
il pleut it is raining

jambon *m.* ham
jardin *m.* garden
jardin publique *m.* park
jaune yellow
je I
jeter to throw
jeune young
jeune fille *f.* girl
joli pretty
jouer to play
jupe *f.* skirt

laid ugly
lapin *m.* rabbit
lancer to throw
large wide
laver to wash
le, les the
leur, leurs their
lever to raise
limonade *f.* lemonade
lit *m.* bed
livre *m.* book
long long

ma, mon, mes my
maison *f.* house
magasin *m.* shop
manger to eat
mari *m.* husband
mauvais bad
méchant naughty, wicked
meilleur better
mener to lead

mère *f.* mother
midi midday
minuit midnight
moins less
montrer to show

nager to swim
neige *f.* snow
nettoyer to clean
nez *m.* nose
noir black
nom *m.* name
non no
notre, nos our
nous we
nouveau new

oiseau *m.* bird
oncle *m.* uncle
orange *f.* orange
orange orange
oreille *f.* ear
où where
oui yes

pain *m.* bread
panier *m.* basket
pantalon *m.* trousers
papeterie *f.* stationer's
parking *m.* carpark
pâtisserie *f.* cake shop
pêcher to fish
père *m.* father
petit small
pharmacie *f.* chemist's shop
pied *m.* foot
piscine *f.* swimming pool
place *f.* square
plage *f.* beach
plonger to dive
poivre *m.* pepper
pomme *f.* apple
porter to carry
poster *m.* poster
poule *f.* hen
préférer to prefer
près de near to

quart *m.* quarter
qui who

radio *f.* radio
raquette *f.* racket
regarder to look at
répéter to repeat

rose *f.* rose
rose pink
rouge red

sa, son, ses his/her
salade *f.* salad
sel *m.* salt
sœur *f.* sister
souris *f.* mouse
sous under
statue *f.* statue
stylo *m.* pen
sucre *m.* sugar
supermarché *m.* super-market
sur on
syndicat d'initiative *f.* tourist office

tableau noir *m.* blackboard
tente *f.* tent
tête *f.* head
thé *m.* tea
théâtre *m.* theatre
ton, ta, tes your
travailler to work
tricher to cheat
tu you

un, une a/an

vache *f.* cow
vase *m.* vase
vélo *m.* bicycle
verre *m.* glass
vert green
viande *f.* meat
vieux old
ville *f.* town
vin *m.* wine
voiture *f.* car
voix *f.* voice
voler to fly
votre, vos your
vrai true

Answers

Le, la, l' (page 4)   A 2 la, the head;   3 l', the money;   4 le, the horse;   5 l', the ambulance;   6 l', the policeman.

B 2 la souris;   3 la maison;   4 la fourchette;   5 l'oreille.

Les (page 5)   A 1 le;   2 la;   3 l';   4 les.

B 2 les fils;   3 le père;   4 le couteau;   5 la femme;   6 les filles;   7 les souris;   8 la voix.

C 2 le nez;   3 les souris;   4 l'agent;   5 les voitures.

Un, une (page 6)   A 2 un;   3 la;   4 une;   5 un;   6 le.

B 2 un vélo;   3 une araignée;   4 une maison.

Des (page 7)   A 2 a policeman;   3 some records;   4 a house;   5 the husband;   6 a bird;   7 some dogs;   8 some sweets.

B 2 les pères;   3 des vaches;   4 les oiseaux;   5 les oreilles;   6 des nez;   7 les têtes;   8 les écoles.

C 2 some cats;   3 a horse;   4 a car;   5 some spiders;   6 some feet!

Un, deux, trois (page 8)   A trente et un trente-deux;   trente-trois;   trente-quatre;   trente-cinq;   trente-six;   trente-sept;   trente-huit;   trente-neuf.

B 2 trente-quatre;   3 quarante-cinq;   4 cinquante et un; 5 soixante-dix;   6 soixante-dix-neuf;   7 quatre-vingt-sept;   8 quatre-vingt-quatorze.

Avoir (pages 9 and 10)   A 2 tu;   3 vous;   4 vous.

B Elle a un livre / un chat / trois disques / une raquette / des bonbons / des crayons.

C 2 oui;   3 non;   4 non.

D 2 Charles n'a pas de vélo.   3 Je n'ai pas de glace.   4 Nous n'avons pas de cousin.

Mon, ma, mes (page 11)   A 2 ma;   3 mes;   4 mon;   5 mon;   6 mes;   7 mes;   8 ma;   9 mes.

B 2 sa sœur;   3 son mari;   4 tes cousines;   5 mes lapins;   6 mes sœurs;   7 son père;   8 mon école

C 1 son oreille;   2 ton école;   3 mon amie;   4 ses frères.

Notre, votre, leur (page 12)   1 2 nos;   3 vos;   4 ton;   5 leur;   6 ton;   7 mon;   8 son;   9 notre;   10 ta.

La famille (page 13)   A 2 quarante;   3 deux;   4 soixante-quinze.

B 2 Elle a treize ans.   3 Elle a trente-six ans.   4 Il a quarante ans.   5 Annick a quinze ans et Sylvie a dix ans.

Adjectives (pages 14 and 15)   A 2 une petite souris;   3 une méchante petite fille;   4 une jolie rose.

B 2 grandes;   3 grand;   4 méchants.

C 2 une bonne école;   3 trois vieilles voitures;   5 la nouvelle voiture.

D 2 une vieille femme;   3 son disque favori;   4 deux belles pommes.

Être (page 16)   A 2 je ne suis pas;   3 vous êtes;   4 vous n'êtes pas;   5 ils ne sont pas;   6 suis-je?   7 sommes-nous?

B 2 X 3 X 4 ✓ 5 X 6 ✓ 7 X 8 ✓ 9 ✓ 10 X 11 X

Bleu, blanc, rouge (page 17)   B 2 ✓ 3 X 4 ✓ 5 X 6 X 7 ✓ 8 ✓

C 2 la vache brune;   3 Le drapeau français est rouge, bleu et blanc. 4 La maison est blanche et noire.

Où? (page 18)   A 2 faux;   3 vrai;   4 vrai.

B 2 L'armoire est derrière le lit.   3 Les balles sont sous la chaise.   4 La raquette est sur le lit.

C 2 Le vin est derrière le panier.   3 L'assiette est entre la fourchette et le couteau.   4 Le sel et le poivre sont devant le panier.

Ce, cette, ces (page 19)   A 2 ces;   3 ce;   4 ces;   5 cet;   6 ces;   7 cette;   8 cet.
B 2 ces filles;   3 cet hôtel;   4 ces maisons;   5 cette école;   6 ces pommes.
Exercises on -er verbs (page 22)
je regarde   I look at, am looking at, do look at
tu regardes   you look at, are looking at, do look at
il, elle, on regarde   he, she, it, one looks at, is looking at, does look at
nous regardons   we look at, are looking at, do look at
vous regardez   you look at, are looking at, do look at
ils, elles regardent   they look at, are looking at, do look at.
B 2 = e;   3=d;   4=a;   5=c.
C 2 We are beginning our homework.   3 He cleans the house.   4 You call the cat.
    5 They are cleaning the blackboard.
D 2 Il pêche.   3 Elle écoute.   4 Ils lavant la voiture.   5 Il porte des fleurs.
Du, de la, de l', des, de, d' (page 23)   A 2 d';   3 du;   4 de la;   5 des;   6 des;   7 de l';
    8 du;   9 de;   10 de.
La ville (page 24)   A 2 vrai;   3 Le parking est à côté du cinéma.   4 La boulangerie est
    en face de la pâtisserie.   5 La statue est au milieu de la place.   6 Le supermarché est
    à côté de la pharmacie et de l'alimentation générale.   7 Le parking est près des
    magasins.
Du, de la, de l', des, de, d' 2 (page 25)   A 2 du;   3 de la;   4 de;   5 de l';   6 des;   7 de la.
B 2 le chien de ma sœur;   3 les voitures des hommes;   4 les oreilles du chat;   5 la
    glace de Jean;   6 la radio de mon ami(e).
Aller (page 26)   A 2 Je vais au parking.   3 Je vais à la piscine.   4 Je vais à la char-
    cuterie.   5 Je vais à l'alimentation générale.   6 Je vais au théâtre.   7 Je vais au
    collège.   8 Je vais au jardin public.   9 Je vàis a l'école.
B 2 vont;   3 vas;   4 allez;   5 va;   6 vas;   7 va;   8 allons.
Faire (page 27)   A 2 Il neige.   3 Il fait du vent.
B 2 fait;   3 font.
Quelle heure est-il? (page 28)   A 2 Il est deux heures et quart.   3 Il est cinq heures et
    demie.   4 Il est sept heures moins vingt.   5 Il est neuf heures moins dix.   6 Il est
    midi.